J
ROG   Rogers

The Christmas pageant.

DATE DUE

THE CAST

Mary—Gwen Matuczek *Joseph*—Francis Corey *Baby Jesus*—Martha Sawyer
Teacher—Lucy Montgomery *Gabriel*—Cybele Dewulf *Innkeepers*—Sarah Mostow,
Nicole Bodrick *Shepherds*—Rosie Ramsey, Nettie Rogers, Daryl Billups
Wise Men—Tory Edwards, Cathy Rhodell, Zach Culley *Angels*—Daisy Noyes,
Brita Rogers, Jordan Springer, Jason Linton, Shannon Keyes, Lindsey Keyes,
Ashley Springer, Emily Goessling, Tanya Linton, Greg Matuczek, Todd Montgomery,
Maggie Montgomery, Leah Sarat, Banjo Sarat *Star Keeper*—Alex Noyes
Stage Technicians—Anna Rogers, Bernie Corey

Music Consultant: Susan Friedlander

For Bernette, who was truly the one behind the scenes.

The CHRISTMAS PAGEANT

by Jacqueline Rogers

GROSSET & DUNLAP · New York

Copyright © 1989 by Jacqueline Rogers. All rights reserved.
Published by Grosset & Dunlap, Inc., a member of The Putnam Publishing Group,
New York. Printed in Singapore. Published simultaneously in Canada.
Library of Congress Catalog Card Number: 88-83046   ISBN 0-448-40151-7
A B C D E F G H I J

Long ago, in a city of Galilee called Nazareth, there lived a young woman, and the woman's name was Mary. Mary was very kind and good, and she was also very special.

One day the angel Gabriel, who was sent by God, came
to Mary and said, "Hail, thou that art highly favored, the Lord
is with thee. Blessed art thou among women."

At first Mary was troubled by the angel's greeting. But
he went on, "Fear not, Mary, for you have found favor with
God. You have been chosen to be the mother of His son. You
shall name him Jesus. He shall be great, and shall be called the
Son of the Highest, and of his kingdom there shall be no end."

Mary did not tell anyone about the visit from the angel. But one person who did know her secret was Joseph, the man she had promised to marry.

An angel had come to Joseph in a dream and told him that Mary was going to bear a son, and that he should call him Jesus, and that he would save people from their sins.

So Joseph took Mary for his wife, because the angel had bid him to.

And it came to pass in those days that there went out a decree that every man must go to his family's city to pay his taxes. Joseph's family had come from Bethlehem.

Although Mary was now great with child, together they began the long journey to Bethlehem, with Mary riding on a donkey and Joseph walking at her side.

Joseph and Mary had to stop many times along the way to rest. When they arrived in Bethlehem, the city was crowded with people who had come to be taxed. Joseph and Mary could find no place to stay.

O Little Town Of Bethlehem

At last a kindly innkeeper saw that Mary was soon to give birth and felt sorry for her and Joseph. "I don't have any room at the inn," said the innkeeper, "but I know a stable where you can stay. At least there you will have a warm place to sleep."

Joseph thanked the innkeeper and filled the stable with clean hay.

And so it was that while they were there, in the stable beside the cows and sheep, the Baby Jesus was born.

Mary wrapped him in swaddling clothes and laid him in a manger filled with straw.

Away In A Manger

Sweetly

Chords: G G C G D7 | D7 G G G G | C G D7 G Am D7 G

1. A - way in a man - ger, No crib for a bed, The lit - tle Lord
2. The cat - tle are low - ing, The poor Ba - by wakes, But lit - tle Lord

Je - sus Laid down His sweet head, The stars in the sky ___ Looked
Je - sus, No cry - ing He makes, I love Thee, Lord Je - sus, Look

down where He lay, The lit - tle Lord Je - sus A - sleep on the hay.
down from the sky, And stay by my cra - dle Till morn - ing is nigh.

On that same night near Bethlehem, there were
shepherds in the field, keeping watch over their flock.
And lo, the angel of the Lord came upon them, and the
glory of the Lord shone round about them, and they
were afraid.

But the angel said to them, "Fear not! For behold,
I bring you good tidings of great joy. Unto you is born
this day a savior who is Christ the Lord. You shall find
the baby wrapped in swaddling clothes, lying in a manger."

Then the sky was suddenly filled with angels, singing and praising God.

Hark, The Herald Angels Sing

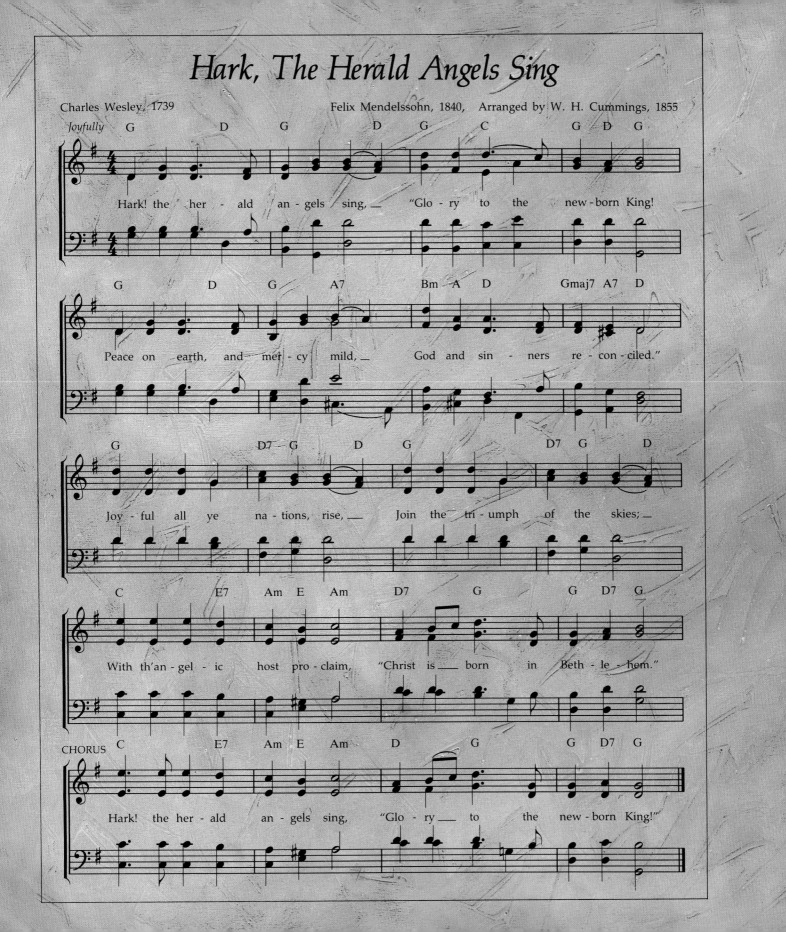

When the angels had gone away into heaven, the shepherds said to one another, "Can this be true? Let us go now to Bethlehem and see this that the angel has told us."

They hurried to the stable and found Mary and Joseph and Baby Jesus, lying in the manger. After this the shepherds traveled about telling everyone what they had seen and heard.

O Come All Ye Faithful

English trans. by
Rev. Frederick Oakeley, 1841

John Francis Wade, 1751

And all those who heard what the shepherds told them were filled with wonder.

One night, behold, there came wise men from the
East to Jerusalem, saying, "Where is he that is born
the king? For we have seen his star in the East and we
have come to worship him. . . ."

And lo, a star appeared and went before them, till
it came and stood over the place where the child was.
And they rejoiced with exceeding great joy.

We Three Kings Of Orient Are

Words and Music by
Rev. John H. Hopkins, Jr., 1857

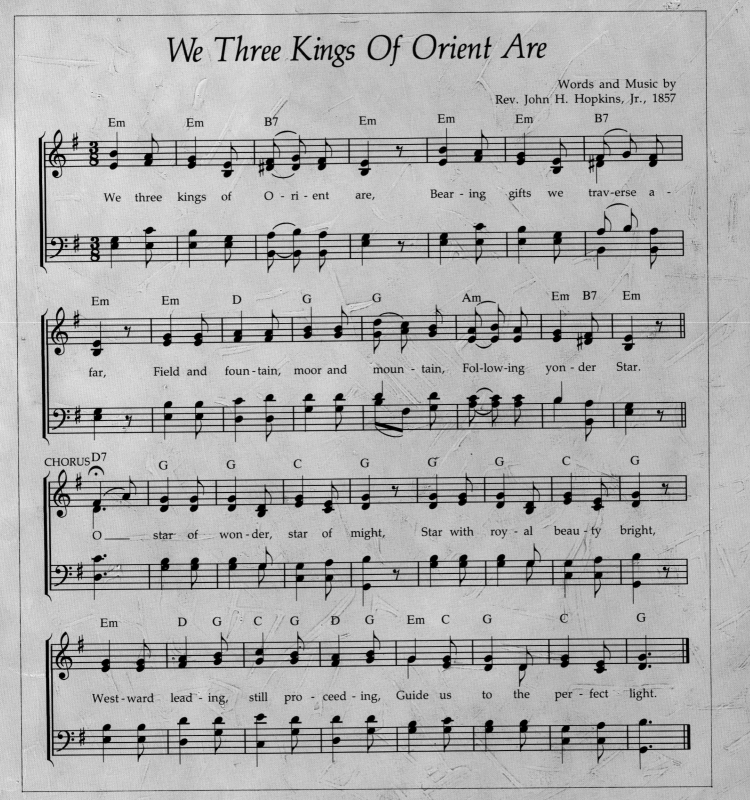

When the wise men came in and saw Jesus, they fell down on their knees and worshipped him. And when they had opened their treasures, they offered him gifts—gold and frankincense and myrrh.

And so it was as the angel had promised. As Jesus grew strong in spirit and wisdom, so he grew in favor with God and man.

Joy To The World